THE 100 METHOD

A 100-Day Transformation Journal

100 Minutes. 100 Days. 1 Goal.

Published by 100 Method Publishing

Printed in the United States of America

First Edition

ISBN: 979-8-9955165-6-9

For permissions, bulk orders, and licensing:
thehundredmethod.com

FIND YOUR WAY

Contents

THE FOUNDATION

THE 100 DAYS

BEYOND DAY 100

WELCOME.

100 Minutes. 100 Days. 1 Goal. This is not a planner. This is a promise.

You didn't pick this up by accident. Something in you is ready — ready to stop circling the goal and start closing in on it.

The 100 Method is simple by design. Every day for the next 100 days, you will dedicate 100 focused minutes to one single goal. Not ten goals. Not a list of habits. One goal. Because clarity is where transformation begins.

Over the next 100 days, you will encounter resistance, doubt, and days when showing up feels impossible. This planner will be there for all of it — the wins, the setbacks, the breakthroughs you didn't see coming. All you have to do is keep showing up.

By Day 100, you will not just have made progress toward your goal. You will have built something no one can take from you — the evidence that you keep your word to yourself.

THIS PLANNER BELONGS TO

Start Date: ______________   End Date (Day 100):

MY GOAL IN ONE LINE:

Write it boldly

THE 100 METHOD™

100
MINUTES

100
DAYS

1
GOAL

The Philosophy

Before you begin, understand what this journey is built on. These are not buzzwords. These are the bones of the work.

---

01 ACCOUNTABILITY

Accountability is not punishment for falling short — it is the honest relationship you build with yourself. It means looking at the truth of where you are without flinching, and choosing to show up anyway. Every day you mark in this planner is an act of accountability. No one is grading you. You are simply keeping your word.

02 CONSISTENCY

Consistency is not perfection. It is showing up even when the conditions aren't perfect — even when you're tired, uninspired, or unsure. The gap between where you are and where you want to be is not talent. It is the accumulation of small, repeated actions. 100 days of consistent effort rewires what you believe is possible for you.

03 DISCIPLINE

Discipline is freedom in disguise. Every time you choose the work over the excuse, you are not restricting yourself — you are expanding what you're capable of. Discipline is not about being hard on yourself. It is about trusting that the version of you on Day 100 is worth protecting today.

04 SELF-LOVE

Self-love is the foundation everything else is built on. It is the belief that you are worth investing in — your time, your focus, your energy. On the hard days, self-love is what keeps you gentle with yourself without letting yourself off the hook. You are doing this because you matter. Don't forget that.

"These four pillars don't just support the goal — they build the person who achieves it."

My Goal

Most people fail not because they lack effort, but because they lack clarity. Before Day 1, get brutally honest about what you are working toward — and why it matters right now.

WHAT IS YOUR GOAL?

WHY DOES THIS GOAL MATTER TO YOU RIGHT NOW?

WHO DO YOU BECOME WHEN YOU ACHIEVE IT?

WHAT HAS STOPPED YOU BEFORE — AND WHAT WILL BE DIFFERENT THIS TIME?

HOW WILL YOU STRUCTURE YOUR 100 MINUTES EACH DAY?

e.g. 2 × 50 min blocks, 4 × 25 min sessions, one focused 100 min block

My Contract

A goal without a commitment is just a wish. What follows is your formal agreement with yourself. Read it. Mean it. Sign it.

— THE 100 METHOD CONTRACT —

I, ___________________________, commit to the following:

I commit to showing up for 100 minutes every day for the next 100 days — not when it is easy, but especially when it is hard.

I commit to one goal. I will not dilute my focus. I understand that clarity is a form of power.

I commit to honesty in this planner. I will record my real days — the wins and the struggles — because the truth is what creates growth.

I commit to treating myself with self-love on hard days, and discipline on easy ones.

I commit to finishing what I start. By Day 100, I will have kept my word to the most important person — myself.

My Goal:

Signed: _____________________ Date:

"The moment you sign this, you are no longer someone who wants the goal. You are someone who is going after it."

My Starting Point

Before the journey changes you, document who you are right now. This page is not a judgment — it is a baseline. On Day 100, you will look back at this and see just how far you have come.

WHERE AM I PHYSICALLY RIGHT NOW?

WHERE AM I MENTALLY AND EMOTIONALLY RIGHT NOW?

WHAT DOES MY CURRENT DAILY ROUTINE LOOK LIKE?

WHAT IS ONE THING I AM LEAVING BEHIND AS I BEGIN THIS JOURNEY?

WHAT DOES SUCCESS LOOK AND FEEL LIKE ON DAY 100?

"You can't know how far you've traveled if you don't mark where you started."

Milestone Intentions

Every 25 days you will pause, zoom out, and check in with your progress. Before you begin, plant seeds for each milestone. What do you hope to have accomplished by each checkpoint?

DAY 25 — *One quarter of the way. What do you hope to have accomplished or shifted?*

DAY 50 — *The halfway mark. What should be noticeably different by now?*

DAY 75 — *Three quarters through. What does momentum feel like at this stage?*

DAY 100 — *The finish line. Paint the picture of what completing this looks like.*

How to Use This Planner

Everything you need to know before Day 1. Read this once, then begin.

Complete the Foundation Section first

Before you touch a daily page, work through pages 3–10. Set your goal, sign your contract, document your starting point. This is not optional — it is the foundation that holds the next 100 days up.

Use one page every single day

Each daily page takes 5–10 minutes — a few minutes in the morning to set your intention, and a few at the end of the day to reflect. The 100-minute block tracker sits in the middle. Fill it in as you go.

Track your 100 minutes honestly

Your 100-minute block is divided into four 25-minute segments. Check each off as you complete it. You can also do 2 × 50 min or any structure that fits your life. The goal is 100 focused minutes on your one goal.

Pause at every Milestone

Days 25, 50, and 75 have dedicated Milestone Check-In pages. Do not skip them. These are the moments you zoom out, measure your growth, and realign with your original intention.

Be honest — always

This planner only works if you tell the truth in it. Did you show up or didn't you? The wins matter. The hard days matter just as much. Honesty in this planner is the most direct path to transformation.

Finish what you start

Every day you open this planner is a vote for who you are becoming. On Day 100, you will have 100 days of evidence that you showed up for yourself. That is the real achievement.

"The method is simple. Your commitment makes it powerful."

100-Day Habit Tracker

Fill in each box the day you complete your 100 minutes. Watch your consistency build into something unshakeable.

1	2	3	4	5	6	7	8	9	10
☐	☐	☐	☐	☐	☐	☐	☐	☐	☐
11	12	13	14	15	16	17	18	19	20
☐	☐	☐	☐	☐	☐	☐	☐	☐	☐
21	22	23	24	**25**	26	27	28	29	30
☐	☐	☐	☐	☐	☐	☐	☐	☐	☐
31	32	33	34	35	36	37	38	39	40
☐	☐	☐	☐	☐	☐	☐	☐	☐	☐
41	42	43	44	45	46	47	48	49	**50**
☐	☐	☐	☐	☐	☐	☐	☐	☐	☐
51	52	53	54	55	56	57	58	59	60
☐	☐	☐	☐	☐	☐	☐	☐	☐	☐
61	62	63	64	65	66	67	68	69	70
☐	☐	☐	☐	☐	☐	☐	☐	☐	☐
71	72	73	74	**75**	76	77	78	79	80
☐	☐	☐	☐	☐	☐	☐	☐	☐	☐
81	82	83	84	85	86	87	88	89	90
☐	☐	☐	☐	☐	☐	☐	☐	☐	☐
91	92	93	94	95	96	97	98	99	**100**
☐	☐	☐	☐	☐	☐	☐	☐	☐	☐

☐ Daily box — check off when you complete 100 minutes   ☐ Gold box — Milestone day (25, 50, 75, 100)

"Every checked box is proof. Build the evidence."

DAY 1

Date:

of 100

TODAY'S INTENTION

In one sentence — what am I here to do today?

MY 100-MINUTE BLOCK

Block 1	Block 2	Block 3	Block 4
25 min	25 min	25 min	25 min
☐ Complete	☐ Complete	☐ Complete	☐ Complete

TODAY'S WIN

One thing — no matter how small.

END-OF-DAY REFLECTION

What happened today? What did I feel? What do I carry into tomorrow?

ENERGY LEVEL TODAY

☐ 1 ☐ 2 ☐ 3 ☐ 4 ☐ 5

Low   High

DID I SHOW UP TODAY?

☐ Yes   ☐ No — and that's okay.

Tomorrow's a new day.

DAY 2

Date:

of 100

TODAY'S INTENTION

In one sentence — what am I here to do today?

MY 100-MINUTE BLOCK

Block 1	**Block 2**	**Block 3**	**Block 4**
25 min	*25 min*	*25 min*	*25 min*
☐ Complete	☐ Complete	☐ Complete	☐ Complete

TODAY'S WIN

One thing — no matter how small.

END-OF-DAY REFLECTION

What happened today? What did I feel? What do I carry into tomorrow?

ENERGY LEVEL TODAY

☐ 1 ☐ 2 ☐ 3 ☐ 4 ☐ 5

Low   High

DID I SHOW UP TODAY?

☐ Yes   ☐ No — and that's okay.

Tomorrow is a new day.

DAY 3

Date:

of 100

TODAY'S INTENTION

In one sentence — what am I here to do today?

MY 100-MINUTE BLOCK

Block 1	**Block 2**	**Block 3**	**Block 4**
25 min	25 min	25 min	25 min
☐ Complete	☐ Complete	☐ Complete	☐ Complete

TODAY'S WIN

One thing — no matter how small.

END-OF-DAY REFLECTION

What happened today? What did I feel? What do I carry into tomorrow?

ENERGY LEVEL TODAY

☐ 1 ☐ 2 ☐ 3 ☐ 4 ☐ 5

Low   High

DID I SHOW UP TODAY?

☐ Yes   ☐ No — and that's okay.

Tomorrow is a new day.

DAY 4

Date:
of 100

TODAY'S INTENTION

In one sentence — what am I here to do today?

MY 100-MINUTE BLOCK

Block 1	Block 2	Block 3	Block 4
25 min	*25 min*	*25 min*	*25 min*
☐ Complete	☐ Complete	☐ Complete	☐ Complete

TODAY'S WIN

One thing — no matter how small.

END-OF-DAY REFLECTION

What happened today? What did I feel? What do I carry into tomorrow?

ENERGY LEVEL TODAY

☐ 1 ☐ 2 ☐ 3 ☐ 4 ☐ 5

Low   High

DID I SHOW UP TODAY?

☐ Yes   ☐ No — and that's okay.

Tomorrow is a new day.

DAY 5

Date:

of 100

TODAY'S INTENTION

In one sentence — what am I here to do today?

MY 100-MINUTE BLOCK

Block 1	**Block 2**	**Block 3**	**Block 4**
25 min	*25 min*	*25 min*	*25 min*
☐ Complete	☐ Complete	☐ Complete	☐ Complete

TODAY'S WIN

One thing — no matter how small.

END-OF-DAY REFLECTION

What happened today? What did I feel? What do I carry into tomorrow?

ENERGY LEVEL TODAY

☐ 1 ☐ 2 ☐ 3 ☐ 4 ☐ 5

Low   High

DID I SHOW UP TODAY?

☐ Yes ☐ No — and that's okay.

Tomorrow is a new day.

DAY 6

Date:

of 100

TODAY'S INTENTION

In one sentence — what am I here to do today?

MY 100-MINUTE BLOCK

Block 1	**Block 2**	**Block 3**	**Block 4**
25 min	*25 min*	*25 min*	*25 min*
☐ Complete	☐ Complete	☐ Complete	☐ Complete

TODAY'S WIN

One thing — no matter how small.

END-OF-DAY REFLECTION

What happened today? What did I feel? What do I carry into tomorrow?

ENERGY LEVEL TODAY

☐ 1 ☐ 2 ☐ 3 ☐ 4 ☐ 5

Low　　　　　High

DID I SHOW UP TODAY?

☐ Yes   ☐ No — and that's okay.

Tomorrow is a new day.

DAY 7

Date:

of 100

TODAY'S INTENTION

In one sentence — what am I here to do today?

MY 100-MINUTE BLOCK

Block 1	**Block 2**	**Block 3**	**Block 4**
25 min	*25 min*	*25 min*	*25 min*
☐ Complete	☐ Complete	☐ Complete	☐ Complete

TODAY'S WIN

One thing — no matter how small.

END-OF-DAY REFLECTION

What happened today? What did I feel? What do I carry into tomorrow?

ENERGY LEVEL TODAY

☐ 1 ☐ 2 ☐ 3 ☐ 4 ☐ 5

Low   High

DID I SHOW UP TODAY?

☐ Yes   ☐ No — and that's okay.

Tomorrow is a new day.

DAY 8

Date:

of 100

TODAY'S INTENTION

In one sentence — what am I here to do today?

MY 100-MINUTE BLOCK

Block 1	Block 2	Block 3	Block 4
25 min	*25 min*	*25 min*	*25 min*
☐ Complete	☐ Complete	☐ Complete	☐ Complete

TODAY'S WIN

One thing — no matter how small.

END-OF-DAY REFLECTION

What happened today? What did I feel? What do I carry into tomorrow?

ENERGY LEVEL TODAY

☐ 1 ☐ 2 ☐ 3 ☐ 4 ☐ 5

Low　　　　High

DID I SHOW UP TODAY?

☐ Yes　☐ No — and that's okay.

Tomorrow is a new day.

DAY 9

Date:
of 100

TODAY'S INTENTION

In one sentence — what am I here to do today?

MY 100-MINUTE BLOCK

Block 1	**Block 2**	**Block 3**	**Block 4**
25 min	*25 min*	*25 min*	*25 min*
☐ Complete	☐ Complete	☐ Complete	☐ Complete

TODAY'S WIN

One thing — no matter how small

END-OF-DAY REFLECTION

What happened today? What did I feel? What do I carry into tomorrow?

ENERGY LEVEL TODAY

☐ 1 ☐ 2 ☐ 3 ☐ 4 ☐ 5
Low　　　　High

DID I SHOW UP TODAY?

☐ Yes ☐ No — and that's okay.
Tomorrow is a new day.

DAY 10

Date:

of 100

TODAY'S INTENTION

In one sentence — what am I here to do today?

MY 100-MINUTE BLOCK

Block 1	Block 2	Block 3	Block 4
25 min	*25 min*	*25 min*	*25 min*
☐ Complete	☐ Complete	☐ Complete	☐ Complete

TODAY'S WIN

One thing — no matter how small.

END-OF-DAY REFLECTION

What happened today? What did I feel? What do I carry into tomorrow?

ENERGY LEVEL TODAY

☐ 1 ☐ 2 ☐ 3 ☐ 4 ☐ 5

Low　　　　High

DID I SHOW UP TODAY?

☐ Yes ☐ No — and that's okay.

Tomorrow is a new day.

DAY 11

Date:

of 100

TODAY'S INTENTION

In one sentence — what am I here to do today?

MY 100-MINUTE BLOCK

Block 1	**Block 2**	**Block 3**	**Block 4**
25 min	25 min	25 min	25 min
☐ Complete	☐ Complete	☐ Complete	☐ Complete

TODAY'S WIN

One thing — no matter how small.

END-OF-DAY REFLECTION

What happened today? What did I feel? What do I carry into tomorrow?

ENERGY LEVEL TODAY

☐ 1 ☐ 2 ☐ 3 ☐ 4 ☐ 5

Low   High

DID I SHOW UP TODAY?

☐ Yes   ☐ No — and that's okay.

Tomorrow is a new day.

DAY 12

Date:

of 100

TODAY'S INTENTION

In one sentence — what am I here to do today?

MY 100-MINUTE BLOCK

Block 1	Block 2	Block 3	Block 4
25 min	*25 min*	*25 min*	*25 min*
☐ Complete	☐ Complete	☐ Complete	☐ Complete

TODAY'S WIN

One thing — no matter how small.

END-OF-DAY REFLECTION

What happened today? What did I feel? What do I carry into tomorrow?

ENERGY LEVEL TODAY

☐ 1 ☐ 2 ☐ 3 ☐ 4 ☐ 5

Low   High

DID I SHOW UP TODAY?

☐ Yes   ☐ No — and that's okay.

Tomorrow is a new day.

DAY 13

Date:

of 100

TODAY'S INTENTION

In one sentence — what am I here to do today?

MY 100-MINUTE BLOCK

Block 1	Block 2	Block 3	Block 4
25 min	25 min	25 min	25 min
☐ Complete	☐ Complete	☐ Complete	☐ Complete

TODAY'S WIN

One thing — no matter how small.

END-OF-DAY REFLECTION

What happened today? What did I feel? What do I carry into tomorrow?

ENERGY LEVEL TODAY

☐ 1 ☐ 2 ☐ 3 ☐ 4 ☐ 5

Low   High

DID I SHOW UP TODAY?

☐ Yes   ☐ No — and that's okay.

Tomorrow is a new day.

DAY 14

Date:

of 100

TODAY'S INTENTION

In one sentence — what am I here to do today?

MY 100-MINUTE BLOCK

Block 1	Block 2	Block 3	Block 4
25 min	*25 min*	*25 min*	*25 min*
☐ Complete	☐ Complete	☐ Complete	☐ Complete

TODAY'S WIN

One thing — no matter how small.

END-OF-DAY REFLECTION

What happened today? What did I feel? What do I carry into tomorrow?

ENERGY LEVEL TODAY

☐ 1 ☐ 2 ☐ 3 ☐ 4 ☐ 5

Low   High

DID I SHOW UP TODAY?

☐ Yes   ☐ No — and that's okay.

Tomorrow is a new day.

DAY 15

Date:

of 100

TODAY'S INTENTION

In one sentence — what am I here to do today?

MY 100-MINUTE BLOCK

Block 1	Block 2	Block 3	Block 4
25 min	25 min	25 min	25 min
☐ Complete	☐ Complete	☐ Complete	☐ Complete

TODAY'S WIN

One thing — no matter how small.

END-OF-DAY REFLECTION

What happened today? What did I feel? What do I carry into tomorrow?

ENERGY LEVEL TODAY

☐ 1 ☐ 2 ☐ 3 ☐ 4 ☐ 5

Low   High

DID I SHOW UP TODAY?

☐ Yes ☐ No — and that's okay.

Tomorrow is a new day.

DAY 16

Date:

of 100

TODAY'S INTENTION

In one sentence — what am I here to do today?

MY 100-MINUTE BLOCK

Block 1	Block 2	Block 3	Block 4
25 min	*25 min*	*25 min*	*25 min*
☐ Complete	☐ Complete	☐ Complete	☐ Complete

TODAY'S WIN

One thing — no matter how small.

END-OF-DAY REFLECTION

What happened today? What did I feel? What do I carry into tomorrow?

ENERGY LEVEL TODAY

☐ 1 ☐ 2 ☐ 3 ☐ 4 ☐ 5

Low　　　　　High

DID I SHOW UP TODAY?

☐ Yes　☐ No — and that's okay.

Tomorrow is a new day.

DAY 17

Date:

of 100

TODAY'S INTENTION

In one sentence — what am I here to do today?

MY 100-MINUTE BLOCK

Block 1	Block 2	Block 3	Block 4
25 min	25 min	25 min	25 min
☐ Complete	☐ Complete	☐ Complete	☐ Complete

TODAY'S WIN

One thing — no matter how small.

END-OF-DAY REFLECTION

What happened today? What did I feel? What do I carry into tomorrow?

ENERGY LEVEL TODAY

☐ 1 ☐ 2 ☐ 3 ☐ 4 ☐ 5

Low   High

DID I SHOW UP TODAY?

☐ Yes   ☐ No — and that's okay.

Tomorrow is a new day.

DAY 18

Date:

of 100

TODAY'S INTENTION

In one sentence — what am I here to do today?

MY 100-MINUTE BLOCK

Block 1	Block 2	Block 3	Block 4
25 min	*25 min*	*25 min*	*25 min*
☐ Complete	☐ Complete	☐ Complete	☐ Complete

TODAY'S WIN

One thing — no matter how small.

END-OF-DAY REFLECTION

What happened today? What did I feel? What do I carry into tomorrow?

ENERGY LEVEL TODAY

☐ 1 ☐ 2 ☐ 3 ☐ 4 ☐ 5

Low   High

DID I SHOW UP TODAY?

☐ Yes   ☐ No — and that's okay.

Tomorrow is a new day.

DAY 19

Date:

of 100

TODAY'S INTENTION

In one sentence — what am I here to do today?

MY 100-MINUTE BLOCK

Block 1	Block 2	Block 3	Block 4
25 min	*25 min*	*25 min*	*25 min*
☐ Complete	☐ Complete	☐ Complete	☐ Complete

TODAY'S WIN

One thing — no matter how small.

END-OF-DAY REFLECTION

What happened today? What did I feel? What do I carry into tomorrow?

ENERGY LEVEL TODAY

☐ 1 ☐ 2 ☐ 3 ☐ 4 ☐ 5

Low　　　　　High

DID I SHOW UP TODAY?

☐ Yes　☐ No — and that's okay.

Tomorrow is a new day.

DAY 20

Date:

of 100

TODAY'S INTENTION

In one sentence — what am I here to do today?

MY 100-MINUTE BLOCK

Block 1	**Block 2**	**Block 3**	**Block 4**
25 min	*25 min*	*25 min*	*25 min*
☐ Complete	☐ Complete	☐ Complete	☐ Complete

TODAY'S WIN

One thing — no matter how small.

END-OF-DAY REFLECTION

What happened today? What did I feel? What do I carry into tomorrow?

ENERGY LEVEL TODAY

☐ 1 ☐ 2 ☐ 3 ☐ 4 ☐ 5

Low   High

DID I SHOW UP TODAY?

☐ Yes   ☐ No — and that's okay.

Tomorrow is a new day.

DAY 21

Date:

of 100

TODAY'S INTENTION

In one sentence — what am I here to do today?

MY 100-MINUTE BLOCK

Block 1	**Block 2**	**Block 3**	**Block 4**
25 min	*25 min*	*25 min*	*25 min*
☐ Complete	☐ Complete	☐ Complete	☐ Complete

TODAY'S WIN

One thing — no matter how small.

END-OF-DAY REFLECTION

What happened today? What did I feel? What do I carry into tomorrow?

ENERGY LEVEL TODAY

☐ 1 ☐ 2 ☐ 3 ☐ 4 ☐ 5

Low　　　　　High

DID I SHOW UP TODAY?

☐ Yes　☐ No — and that's okay.

Tomorrow is a new day.

DAY 22

Date:

of 100

TODAY'S INTENTION

In one sentence — what am I here to do today?

MY 100-MINUTE BLOCK

Block 1	Block 2	Block 3	Block 4
25 min	*25 min*	*25 min*	*25 min*
☐ Complete	☐ Complete	☐ Complete	☐ Complete

TODAY'S WIN

One thing — no matter how small.

END-OF-DAY REFLECTION

What happened today? What did I feel? What do I carry into tomorrow?

ENERGY LEVEL TODAY

☐ 1 ☐ 2 ☐ 3 ☐ 4 ☐ 5

Low   High

DID I SHOW UP TODAY?

☐ Yes   ☐ No — and that's okay.

Tomorrow is a new day.

DAY 23

Date:

of 100

TODAY'S INTENTION

In one sentence — what am I here to do today?

MY 100-MINUTE BLOCK

Block 1	Block 2	Block 3	Block 4
25 min	*25 min*	*25 min*	*25 min*
☐ Complete	☐ Complete	☐ Complete	☐ Complete

TODAY'S WIN

One thing — no matter how small.

END-OF-DAY REFLECTION

What happened today? What did I feel? What do I carry into tomorrow?

ENERGY LEVEL TODAY

☐ 1 ☐ 2 ☐ 3 ☐ 4 ☐ 5

Low　　　　　High

DID I SHOW UP TODAY?

☐ Yes　☐ No — and that's okay.

Tomorrow is a new day.

DAY 24

Date:

of 100

TODAY'S INTENTION

In one sentence — what am I here to do today?

MY 100-MINUTE BLOCK

Block 1	Block 2	Block 3	Block 4
25 min	*25 min*	*25 min*	*25 min*
☐ Complete	☐ Complete	☐ Complete	☐ Complete

TODAY'S WIN

One thing — no matter how small.

END-OF-DAY REFLECTION

What happened today? What did I feel? What do I carry into tomorrow?

ENERGY LEVEL TODAY

☐ 1　☐ 2　☐ 3　☐ 4　☐ 5

Low　　　　High

DID I SHOW UP TODAY?

☐ Yes　☐ No — and that's okay.

Tomorrow is a new day.

DAY 25

"Twenty-five days in. You showed up when it was new, when it was exciting, and when it started getting hard. That is not nothing. That is everything."

THE 100 METHOD™

DAY 25 OF 100

MILESTONE CHECK-IN

Date:

AM I STILL ALIGNED WITH MY ORIGINAL GOAL? WHAT HAS SHIFTED?

WHAT HAS CHANGED IN ME SO FAR — EVEN IF I CAN'T FULLY SEE IT YET?

WHAT DO I NEED TO RELEASE OR ADJUST GOING FORWARD?

ONE THING I'M PROUD OF THAT I DIDN'T EXPECT:

MY INTENTION FOR THE NEXT 25 DAYS:

"25 days in. Keep going. The best is still ahead."

DAY 26

Date:

of 100

TODAY'S INTENTION

In one sentence — what am I here to do today?

MY 100-MINUTE BLOCK

Block 1	**Block 2**	**Block 3**	**Block 4**
25 min	25 min	25 min	25 min
☐ Complete	☐ Complete	☐ Complete	☐ Complete

TODAY'S WIN

One thing — no matter how small.

END-OF-DAY REFLECTION

What happened today? What did I feel? What do I carry into tomorrow?

ENERGY LEVEL TODAY

☐ 1 ☐ 2 ☐ 3 ☐ 4 ☐ 5

Low   High

DID I SHOW UP TODAY?

☐ Yes   ☐ No — and that's okay.

Tomorrow is a new day.

DAY 27

Date:

of 100

TODAY'S INTENTION

In one sentence — what am I here to do today?

MY 100-MINUTE BLOCK

Block 1	Block 2	Block 3	Block 4
25 min	*25 min*	*25 min*	*25 min*
☐ Complete	☐ Complete	☐ Complete	☐ Complete

TODAY'S WIN

One thing — no matter how small.

END-OF-DAY REFLECTION

What happened today? What did I feel? What do I carry into tomorrow?

ENERGY LEVEL TODAY

☐ 1 ☐ 2 ☐ 3 ☐ 4 ☐ 5

Low   High

DID I SHOW UP TODAY?

☐ Yes   ☐ No — and that's okay.

Tomorrow is a new day.

DAY 28

Date:

of 100

TODAY'S INTENTION

In one sentence — what am I here to do today?

MY 100-MINUTE BLOCK

Block 1	**Block 2**	**Block 3**	**Block 4**
25 min	25 min	25 min	25 min
☐ Complete	☐ Complete	☐ Complete	☐ Complete

TODAY'S WIN

One thing — no matter how small.

END-OF-DAY REFLECTION

What happened today? What did I feel? What do I carry into tomorrow?

ENERGY LEVEL TODAY

☐ 1 ☐ 2 ☐ 3 ☐ 4 ☐ 5

Low　　　　High

DID I SHOW UP TODAY?

☐ Yes　☐ No — and that's okay.

Tomorrow is a new day.

DAY 29

Date:

of 100

TODAY'S INTENTION

In one sentence — what am I here to do today?

MY 100-MINUTE BLOCK

Block 1	Block 2	Block 3	Block 4
25 min	*25 min*	*25 min*	*25 min*
☐ Complete	☐ Complete	☐ Complete	☐ Complete

TODAY'S WIN

One thing — no matter how small.

END-OF-DAY REFLECTION

What happened today? What did I feel? What do I carry into tomorrow?

ENERGY LEVEL TODAY

☐ 1　☐ 2　☐ 3　☐ 4　☐ 5

Low　　　　　High

DID I SHOW UP TODAY?

☐ Yes　☐ No — and that's okay.

Tomorrow is a new day.

DAY 30

Date:

of 100

TODAY'S INTENTION

In one sentence — what am I here to do today?

MY 100-MINUTE BLOCK

Block 1	Block 2	Block 3	Block 4
25 min	25 min	25 min	25 min
☐ Complete	☐ Complete	☐ Complete	☐ Complete

TODAY'S WIN

One thing — no matter how small.

END-OF-DAY REFLECTION

What happened today? What did I feel? What do I carry into tomorrow?

ENERGY LEVEL TODAY

☐ 1 ☐ 2 ☐ 3 ☐ 4 ☐ 5

Low   High

DID I SHOW UP TODAY?

☐ Yes ☐ No — and that's okay.

Tomorrow is a new day.

DAY 31

Date:

of 100

TODAY'S INTENTION

In one sentence — what am I here to do today?

MY 100-MINUTE BLOCK

Block 1	Block 2	Block 3	Block 4
25 min	25 min	25 min	25 min
☐ Complete	☐ Complete	☐ Complete	☐ Complete

TODAY'S WIN

One thing — no matter how small.

END-OF-DAY REFLECTION

What happened today? What did I feel? What do I carry into tomorrow?

ENERGY LEVEL TODAY

☐ 1 ☐ 2 ☐ 3 ☐ 4 ☐ 5

Low   High

DID I SHOW UP TODAY?

☐ Yes   ☐ No — and that's okay.

Tomorrow is a new day.

DAY 32

Date:

of 100

TODAY'S INTENTION

In one sentence — what am I here to do today?

MY 100-MINUTE BLOCK

Block 1	**Block 2**	**Block 3**	**Block 4**
25 min	25 min	25 min	25 min
☐ Complete	☐ Complete	☐ Complete	☐ Complete

TODAY'S WIN

One thing — no matter how small.

END-OF-DAY REFLECTION

What happened today? What did I feel? What do I carry into tomorrow?

ENERGY LEVEL TODAY

☐ 1 ☐ 2 ☐ 3 ☐ 4 ☐ 5

Low　　　　　High

DID I SHOW UP TODAY?

☐ Yes　☐ No — and that's okay.

Tomorrow is a new day.

DAY 33

Date:

of 100

TODAY'S INTENTION

In one sentence — what am I here to do today?

MY 100-MINUTE BLOCK

Block 1	Block 2	Block 3	Block 4
25 min	*25 min*	*25 min*	*25 min*
☐ Complete	☐ Complete	☐ Complete	☐ Complete

TODAY'S WIN

One thing — no matter how small.

END-OF-DAY REFLECTION

What happened today? What did I feel? What do I carry into tomorrow?

ENERGY LEVEL TODAY

☐ 1 ☐ 2 ☐ 3 ☐ 4 ☐ 5

Low   High

DID I SHOW UP TODAY?

☐ Yes   ☐ No — and that's okay.

Tomorrow is a new day.

DAY 34

Date:

of 100

TODAY'S INTENTION

In one sentence — what am I here to do today?

MY 100-MINUTE BLOCK

Block 1	Block 2	Block 3	Block 4
25 min	*25 min*	*25 min*	*25 min*
☐ Complete	☐ Complete	☐ Complete	☐ Complete

TODAY'S WIN

One thing — no matter how small.

END-OF-DAY REFLECTION

What happened today? What did I feel? What do I carry into tomorrow?

ENERGY LEVEL TODAY

☐ 1 ☐ 2 ☐ 3 ☐ 4 ☐ 5

Low　　　　　High

DID I SHOW UP TODAY?

☐ Yes　☐ No — and that's okay.

Tomorrow is a new day.

DAY 35

Date:

of 100

TODAY'S INTENTION

In one sentence — what am I here to do today?

MY 100-MINUTE BLOCK

Block 1	Block 2	Block 3	Block 4
25 min	*25 min*	*25 min*	*25 min*
☐ Complete	☐ Complete	☐ Complete	☐ Complete

TODAY'S WIN

One thing — no matter how small.

END-OF-DAY REFLECTION

What happened today? What did I feel? What do I carry into tomorrow?

ENERGY LEVEL TODAY

☐ 1 ☐ 2 ☐ 3 ☐ 4 ☐ 5

Low   High

DID I SHOW UP TODAY?

☐ Yes ☐ No — and that's okay.

Tomorrow is a new day.

DAY 36

Date:

of 100

TODAY'S INTENTION

In one sentence — what am I here to do today?

MY 100-MINUTE BLOCK

Block 1	**Block 2**	**Block 3**	**Block 4**
25 min	25 min	25 min	25 min
☐ Complete	☐ Complete	☐ Complete	☐ Complete

TODAY'S WIN

One thing — no matter how small.

END-OF-DAY REFLECTION

What happened today? What did I feel? What do I carry into tomorrow?

ENERGY LEVEL TODAY

☐ 1 ☐ 2 ☐ 3 ☐ 4 ☐ 5

Low   High

DID I SHOW UP TODAY?

☐ Yes   ☐ No — and that's okay.

Tomorrow is a new day.

DAY 37

Date:

of 100

TODAY'S INTENTION

In one sentence — what am I here to do today?

MY 100-MINUTE BLOCK

Block 1	Block 2	Block 3	Block 4
25 min	*25 min*	*25 min*	*25 min*
☐ Complete	☐ Complete	☐ Complete	☐ Complete

TODAY'S WIN

One thing -- no matter how small.

END-OF-DAY REFLECTION

What happened today? What did I feel? What do I carry into tomorrow?

ENERGY LEVEL TODAY

☐ 1 ☐ 2 ☐ 3 ☐ 4 ☐ 5

Low   High

DID I SHOW UP TODAY?

☐ Yes ☐ No — and that's okay.

Tomorrow is a new day.

DAY 38

Date:

of 100

TODAY'S INTENTION

In one sentence — what am I here to do today?

MY 100-MINUTE BLOCK

Block 1	Block 2	Block 3	Block 4
25 min	25 min	25 min	25 min
☐ Complete	☐ Complete	☐ Complete	☐ Complete

TODAY'S WIN

One thing — no matter how small.

END-OF-DAY REFLECTION

What happened today? What did I feel? What do I carry into tomorrow?

ENERGY LEVEL TODAY

☐ 1 ☐ 2 ☐ 3 ☐ 4 ☐ 5

Low   High

DID I SHOW UP TODAY?

☐ Yes   ☐ No — and that's okay.

Tomorrow is a new day.

DAY 39

Date:

of 100

TODAY'S INTENTION

In one sentence — what am I here to do today?

MY 100-MINUTE BLOCK

Block 1	Block 2	Block 3	Block 4
25 min	*25 min*	*25 min*	*25 min*
☐ Complete	☐ Complete	☐ Complete	☐ Complete

TODAY'S WIN

One thing — no matter how small.

END-OF-DAY REFLECTION

What happened today? What did I feel? What do I carry into tomorrow?

ENERGY LEVEL TODAY

☐ 1 ☐ 2 ☐ 3 ☐ 4 ☐ 5

Low   High

DID I SHOW UP TODAY?

☐ Yes   ☐ No — and that's okay.

Tomorrow is a new day.

DAY 40

Date:

of 100

TODAY'S INTENTION

In one sentence — what am I here to do today?

MY 100-MINUTE BLOCK

Block 1	**Block 2**	**Block 3**	**Block 4**
25 min	25 min	25 min	25 min
☐ Complete	☐ Complete	☐ Complete	☐ Complete

TODAY'S WIN

One thing — no matter how small.

END-OF-DAY REFLECTION

What happened today? What did I feel? What do I carry into tomorrow?

ENERGY LEVEL TODAY

☐ 1 ☐ 2 ☐ 3 ☐ 4 ☐ 5

Low   High

DID I SHOW UP TODAY?

☐ Yes ☐ No — and that's okay.

Tomorrow is a new day.

DAY 41

Date:

of 100

TODAY'S INTENTION

In one sentence — what am I here to do today?

MY 100-MINUTE BLOCK

Block 1	Block 2	Block 3	Block 4
25 min	*25 min*	*25 min*	*25 min*
☐ Complete	☐ Complete	☐ Complete	☐ Complete

TODAY'S WIN

One thing — no matter how small.

END-OF-DAY REFLECTION

What happened today? What did I feel? What do I carry into tomorrow?

ENERGY LEVEL TODAY

☐ 1 ☐ 2 ☐ 3 ☐ 4 ☐ 5

Low   High

DID I SHOW UP TODAY?

☐ Yes   ☐ No — and that's okay.

Tomorrow is a new day.

DAY 42

Date:

of 100

TODAY'S INTENTION

In one sentence — what am I here to do today?

MY 100-MINUTE BLOCK

Block 1	**Block 2**	**Block 3**	**Block 4**
25 min	25 min	25 min	25 min
☐ Complete	☐ Complete	☐ Complete	☐ Complete

TODAY'S WIN

One thing — no matter how small.

END-OF-DAY REFLECTION

What happened today? What did I feel? What do I carry into tomorrow?

ENERGY LEVEL TODAY

☐ 1 ☐ 2 ☐ 3 ☐ 4 ☐ 5

Low   High

DID I SHOW UP TODAY?

☐ Yes   ☐ No — and that's okay.

Tomorrow is a new day.

DAY 43

Date:

of 100

TODAY'S INTENTION

In one sentence — what am I here to do today?

MY 100-MINUTE BLOCK

Block 1	Block 2	Block 3	Block 4
25 min	*25 min*	*25 min*	*25 min*
☐ Complete	☐ Complete	☐ Complete	☐ Complete

TODAY'S WIN

One thing — no matter how small.

END-OF-DAY REFLECTION

What happened today? What did I feel? What do I carry into tomorrow?

ENERGY LEVEL TODAY

☐ 1 ☐ 2 ☐ 3 ☐ 4 ☐ 5

Low   High

DID I SHOW UP TODAY?

☐ Yes   ☐ No — and that's okay.
Tomorrow is a new day.

DAY 44

Date:

of 100

TODAY'S INTENTION

In one sentence — what am I here to do today?

MY 100-MINUTE BLOCK

Block 1	Block 2	Block 3	Block 4
25 min	25 min	25 min	25 min
☐ Complete	☐ Complete	☐ Complete	☐ Complete

TODAY'S WIN

One thing — no matter how small.

END-OF-DAY REFLECTION

What happened today? What did I feel? What do I carry into tomorrow?

ENERGY LEVEL TODAY

☐ 1 ☐ 2 ☐ 3 ☐ 4 ☐ 5

Low   High

DID I SHOW UP TODAY?

☐ Yes   ☐ No — and that's okay.

Tomorrow is a new day.

DAY 45

Date:

of 100

TODAY'S INTENTION

In one sentence — what am I here to do today?

MY 100-MINUTE BLOCK

Block 1	**Block 2**	**Block 3**	**Block 4**
25 min	*25 min*	*25 min*	*25 min*
☐ Complete	☐ Complete	☐ Complete	☐ Complete

TODAY'S WIN

One thing — no matter how small.

END-OF-DAY REFLECTION

What happened today? What did I feel? What do I carry into tomorrow?

ENERGY LEVEL TODAY

☐ 1 ☐ 2 ☐ 3 ☐ 4 ☐ 5

Low   High

DID I SHOW UP TODAY?

☐ Yes   ☐ No — and that's okay.

Tomorrow is a new day.

DAY 46

Date:

of 100

TODAY'S INTENTION

In one sentence — what am I here to do today?

MY 100-MINUTE BLOCK

Block 1	Block 2	Block 3	Block 4
25 min	25 min	25 min	25 min
☐ Complete	☐ Complete	☐ Complete	☐ Complete

TODAY'S WIN

One thing — no matter how small.

END-OF-DAY REFLECTION

What happened today? What did I feel? What do I carry into tomorrow?

ENERGY LEVEL TODAY

☐ 1 ☐ 2 ☐ 3 ☐ 4 ☐ 5

Low　　　　　High

DID I SHOW UP TODAY?

☐ Yes ☐ No — and that's okay.

Tomorrow is a new day.

DAY 47

Date:

of 100

TODAY'S INTENTION

In one sentence — what am I here to do today?

MY 100-MINUTE BLOCK

Block 1	Block 2	Block 3	Block 4
25 min	*25 min*	*25 min*	*25 min*
☐ Complete	☐ Complete	☐ Complete	☐ Complete

TODAY'S WIN

One thing — no matter how small.

END-OF-DAY REFLECTION

What happened today? What did I feel? What do I carry into tomorrow?

ENERGY LEVEL TODAY

☐ 1 ☐ 2 ☐ 3 ☐ 4 ☐ 5

Low   High

DID I SHOW UP TODAY?

☐ Yes   ☐ No — and that's okay.

Tomorrow is a new day.

DAY 48

Date:

of 100

TODAY'S INTENTION

In one sentence — what am I here to do today?

MY 100-MINUTE BLOCK

Block 1	**Block 2**	**Block 3**	**Block 4**
25 min	*25 min*	*25 min*	*25 min*
☐ Complete	☐ Complete	☐ Complete	☐ Complete

TODAY'S WIN

One thing — no matter how small.

END-OF-DAY REFLECTION

What happened today? What did I feel? What do I carry into tomorrow?

ENERGY LEVEL TODAY

☐ 1 ☐ 2 ☐ 3 ☐ 4 ☐ 5

Low *High*

DID I SHOW UP TODAY?

☐ Yes ☐ No — and that's okay.

Tomorrow's a new day.

DAY 49

Date:

of 100

TODAY'S INTENTION

In one sentence — what am I here to do today?

MY 100-MINUTE BLOCK

Block 1 *25 min* ☐ Complete	**Block 2** *25 min* ☐ Complete	**Block 3** *25 min* ☐ Complete	**Block 4** *25 min* ☐ Complete

TODAY'S WIN

One thing — no matter how small.

END-OF-DAY REFLECTION

What happened today? What did I feel? What do I carry into tomorrow?

ENERGY LEVEL TODAY

☐ 1　☐ 2　☐ 3　☐ 4　☐ 5

Low　　　High

DID I SHOW UP TODAY?

☐ Yes　☐ No — and that's okay.

Tomorrow is a new day.

DAY 50

"*Halfway. Look back at who started this journey. Look forward at who is waiting on the other side. The distance between them is built one day at a time.*"

DAY 50 OF 100

MILESTONE CHECK-IN

Date:

AM I STILL ALIGNED WITH MY ORIGINAL GOAL? WHAT HAS SHIFTED?

WHAT HAS CHANGED IN ME SO FAR — EVEN IF I CAN'T FULLY SEE IT YET?

WHAT DO I NEED TO RELEASE OR ADJUST GOING FORWARD?

ONE THING I'M PROUD OF THAT I DIDN'T EXPECT:

MY INTENTION FOR THE NEXT 25 DAYS:

"50 days in. Keep going. The best is still ahead."

DAY 51

Date:

of 100

TODAY'S INTENTION

In one sentence — what am I here to do today?

MY 100-MINUTE BLOCK

Block 1	**Block 2**	**Block 3**	**Block 4**
25 min	*25 min*	*25 min*	*25 min*
☐ Complete	☐ Complete	☐ Complete	☐ Complete

TODAY'S WIN

One thing — no matter how small.

END-OF-DAY REFLECTION

What happened today? What did I feel? What do I carry into tomorrow?

ENERGY LEVEL TODAY

☐ 1 ☐ 2 ☐ 3 ☐ 4 ☐ 5

Low   High

DID I SHOW UP TODAY?

☐ Yes ☐ No — and that's okay.

Tomorrow is a new day.

DAY 52

Date:

of 100

TODAY'S INTENTION

In one sentence — what am I here to do today?

MY 100-MINUTE BLOCK

Block 1	Block 2	Block 3	Block 4
25 min	*25 min*	*25 min*	*25 min*
☐ Complete	☐ Complete	☐ Complete	☐ Complete

TODAY'S WIN

One thing — no matter how small.

END-OF-DAY REFLECTION

What happened today? What did I feel? What do I carry into tomorrow?

ENERGY LEVEL TODAY

☐ 1 ☐ 2 ☐ 3 ☐ 4 ☐ 5

Low　　　　High

DID I SHOW UP TODAY?

☐ Yes　☐ No — and that's okay.

Tomorrow is a new day.

DAY 53

Date:

of 100

TODAY'S INTENTION

In one sentence — what am I here to do today?

MY 100-MINUTE BLOCK

Block 1	Block 2	Block 3	Block 4
25 min	25 min	25 min	25 min
☐ Complete	☐ Complete	☐ Complete	☐ Complete

TODAY'S WIN

One thing — no matter how small.

END-OF-DAY REFLECTION

What happened today? What did I feel? What do I carry into tomorrow?

ENERGY LEVEL TODAY

☐ 1　☐ 2　☐ 3　☐ 4　☐ 5

Low　　　　High

DID I SHOW UP TODAY?

☐ Yes　☐ No — and that's okay.

Tomorrow is a new day.

DAY 54

Date:

of 100

TODAY'S INTENTION

In one sentence — what am I here to do today?

MY 100-MINUTE BLOCK

Block 1	Block 2	Block 3	Block 4
25 min	*25 min*	*25 min*	*25 min*
☐ Complete	☐ Complete	☐ Complete	☐ Complete

TODAY'S WIN

One thing — no matter how small.

END-OF-DAY REFLECTION

What happened today? What did I feel? What do I carry into tomorrow?

ENERGY LEVEL TODAY

☐ 1 ☐ 2 ☐ 3 ☐ 4 ☐ 5

Low   High

DID I SHOW UP TODAY?

☐ Yes   ☐ No — and that's okay.

Tomorrow is a new day.

DAY 55

Date:

of 100

TODAY'S INTENTION

In one sentence — what am I here to do today?

MY 100-MINUTE BLOCK

Block 1	Block 2	Block 3	Block 4
25 min	25 min	25 min	25 min
☐ Complete	☐ Complete	☐ Complete	☐ Complete

TODAY'S WIN

One thing — no matter how small.

END-OF-DAY REFLECTION

What happened today? What did I feel? What do I carry into tomorrow?

ENERGY LEVEL TODAY

☐ 1　☐ 2　☐ 3　☐ 4　☐ 5

Low　　　　　　High

DID I SHOW UP TODAY?

☐ Yes　☐ No — and that's okay.

Tomorrow is a new day.

DAY 56

Date:

of 100

TODAY'S INTENTION

In one sentence — what am I here to do today?

MY 100-MINUTE BLOCK

Block 1	Block 2	Block 3	Block 4
25 min	*25 min*	*25 min*	*25 min*
☐ Complete	☐ Complete	☐ Complete	☐ Complete

TODAY'S WIN

One thing — no matter how small.

END-OF-DAY REFLECTION

What happened today? What did I feel? What do I carry into tomorrow?

ENERGY LEVEL TODAY

☐ 1 ☐ 2 ☐ 3 ☐ 4 ☐ 5

Low　　　　High

DID I SHOW UP TODAY?

☐ Yes　☐ No — and that's okay.

Tomorrow is a new day.

DAY 57

Date:

of 100

TODAY'S INTENTION

In one sentence — what am I here to do today?

MY 100-MINUTE BLOCK

Block 1	Block 2	Block 3	Block 4
25 min	25 min	25 min	25 min
☐ Complete	☐ Complete	☐ Complete	☐ Complete

TODAY'S WIN

One thing — no matter how small.

END-OF-DAY REFLECTION

What happened today? What did I feel? What do I carry into tomorrow?

ENERGY LEVEL TODAY

☐ 1 ☐ 2 ☐ 3 ☐ 4 ☐ 5

Low   High

DID I SHOW UP TODAY?

☐ Yes   ☐ No — and that's okay.

Tomorrow is a new day.

DAY 58

Date:

of 100

TODAY'S INTENTION

In one sentence — what am I here to do today?

MY 100-MINUTE BLOCK

Block 1 25 min	Block 2 25 min	Block 3 25 min	Block 4 25 min
☐ Complete	☐ Complete	☐ Complete	☐ Complete

TODAY'S WIN

One thing — no matter how small.

END-OF-DAY REFLECTION

What happened today? What did I feel? What do I carry into tomorrow?

ENERGY LEVEL TODAY

☐ 1 ☐ 2 ☐ 3 ☐ 4 ☐ 5

Low High

DID I SHOW UP TODAY?

☐ Yes ☐ No — and that's okay.

Tomorrow is a new day.

DAY 59

Date:

of 100

TODAY'S INTENTION

In one sentence — what am I here to do today?

MY 100-MINUTE BLOCK

Block 1	Block 2	Block 3	Block 4
25 min	25 min	25 min	25 min
☐ Complete	☐ Complete	☐ Complete	☐ Complete

TODAY'S WIN

One thing — no matter how small

END-OF-DAY REFLECTION

What happened today? What did I feel? What do I carry into tomorrow?

ENERGY LEVEL TODAY

☐ 1 ☐ 2 ☐ 3 ☐ 4 ☐ 5

Low   High

DID I SHOW UP TODAY?

☐ Yes   ☐ No — and that's okay.

Tomorrow is a new day

DAY 60

Date:

of 100

TODAY'S INTENTION

In one sentence — what am I here to do today?

MY 100-MINUTE BLOCK

Block 1 *25 min*	**Block 2** *25 min*	**Block 3** *25 min*	**Block 4** *25 min*
☐ Complete	☐ Complete	☐ Complete	☐ Complete

TODAY'S WIN

One thing — no matter how small.

END-OF-DAY REFLECTION

What happened today? What did I feel? What do I carry into tomorrow?

ENERGY LEVEL TODAY

☐ 1 ☐ 2 ☐ 3 ☐ 4 ☐ 5

Low   High

DID I SHOW UP TODAY?

☐ Yes   ☐ No — and that's okay.

Tomorrow is a new day.

DAY 61

Date:

of 100

TODAY'S INTENTION

In one sentence — what am I here to do today?

MY 100-MINUTE BLOCK

Block 1	Block 2	Block 3	Block 4
25 min	25 min	25 min	25 min
☐ Complete	☐ Complete	☐ Complete	☐ Complete

TODAY'S WIN

One thing — no matter how small.

END-OF-DAY REFLECTION

What happened today? What did I feel? What do I carry into tomorrow?

ENERGY LEVEL TODAY

☐ 1 ☐ 2 ☐ 3 ☐ 4 ☐ 5

Low   High

DID I SHOW UP TODAY?

☐ Yes ☐ No — and that's okay.

Tomorrow is a new day.

DAY 62

Date:

of 100

TODAY'S INTENTION

In one sentence — what am I here to do today?

MY 100-MINUTE BLOCK

Block 1	Block 2	Block 3	Block 4
25 min	*25 min*	*25 min*	*25 min*
☐ Complete	☐ Complete	☐ Complete	☐ Complete

TODAY'S WIN

One thing — no matter how small.

END-OF-DAY REFLECTION

What happened today? What did I feel? What do I carry into tomorrow?

ENERGY LEVEL TODAY

☐ 1 ☐ 2 ☐ 3 ☐ 4 ☐ 5

Low   High

DID I SHOW UP TODAY?

☐ Yes   ☐ No — and that's okay.

Tomorrow is a new day.

DAY 63

Date:

of 100

TODAY'S INTENTION

In one sentence — what am I here to do today?

MY 100-MINUTE BLOCK

Block 1	Block 2	Block 3	Block 4
25 min	*25 min*	*25 min*	*25 min*
☐ Complete	☐ Complete	☐ Complete	☐ Complete

TODAY'S WIN

One thing — no matter how small.

END-OF-DAY REFLECTION

What happened today? What did I feel? What do I carry into tomorrow?

ENERGY LEVEL TODAY

☐ 1　☐ 2　☐ 3　☐ 4　☐ 5

Low　　　High

DID I SHOW UP TODAY?

☐ Yes　☐ No — and that's okay.

Tomorrow is a new day.

DAY 64

Date:

of 100

TODAY'S INTENTION

In one sentence — what am I here to do today?

MY 100-MINUTE BLOCK

Block 1	Block 2	Block 3	Block 4
25 min	*25 min*	*25 min*	*25 min*
☐ Complete	☐ Complete	☐ Complete	☐ Complete

TODAY'S WIN

One thing — no matter how small.

END-OF-DAY REFLECTION

What happened today? What did I feel? What do I carry into tomorrow?

ENERGY LEVEL TODAY

☐ 1 ☐ 2 ☐ 3 ☐ 4 ☐ 5

Low　　　　High

DID I SHOW UP TODAY?

☐ Yes   ☐ No — and that's okay.

Tomorrow is a new day.

DAY 65

Date:

of 100

TODAY'S INTENTION

In one sentence — what am I here to do today?

MY 100-MINUTE BLOCK

Block 1	**Block 2**	**Block 3**	**Block 4**
25 min	25 min	25 min	25 min
☐ Complete	☐ Complete	☐ Complete	☐ Complete

TODAY'S WIN

One thing — no matter how small.

END-OF-DAY REFLECTION

What happened today? What did I feel? What do I carry into tomorrow?

ENERGY LEVEL TODAY

☐ 1 ☐ 2 ☐ 3 ☐ 4 ☐ 5

Low   High

DID I SHOW UP TODAY?

☐ Yes   ☐ No — and that's okay.

Tomorrow is a new day.

DAY 66

Date:

of 100

TODAY'S INTENTION

In one sentence — what am I here to do today?

MY 100-MINUTE BLOCK

Block 1	**Block 2**	**Block 3**	**Block 4**
25 min	*25 min*	*25 min*	*25 min*
☐ Complete	☐ Complete	☐ Complete	☐ Complete

TODAY'S WIN

One thing — no matter how small.

END-OF-DAY REFLECTION

What happened today? What did I feel? What do I carry into tomorrow?

ENERGY LEVEL TODAY

☐ 1 ☐ 2 ☐ 3 ☐ 4 ☐ 5

Low   High

DID I SHOW UP TODAY?

☐ Yes   ☐ No — and that's okay.

Tomorrow is a new day.

DAY 67

Date:

of 100

TODAY'S INTENTION

In one sentence — what am I here to do today?

MY 100-MINUTE BLOCK

Block 1	Block 2	Block 3	Block 4
25 min	25 min	25 min	25 min
☐ Complete	☐ Complete	☐ Complete	☐ Complete

TODAY'S WIN

One thing — no matter how small.

END-OF-DAY REFLECTION

What happened today? What did I feel? What do I carry into tomorrow?

ENERGY LEVEL TODAY

☐ 1 ☐ 2 ☐ 3 ☐ 4 ☐ 5

Low　　　　　High

DID I SHOW UP TODAY?

☐ Yes　☐ No — and that's okay.

Tomorrow is a new day.

DAY 68

Date:

of 100

TODAY'S INTENTION

In one sentence — what am I here to do today?

MY 100-MINUTE BLOCK

Block 1	Block 2	Block 3	Block 4
25 min	*25 min*	*25 min*	*25 min*
☐ Complete	☐ Complete	☐ Complete	☐ Complete

TODAY'S WIN

One thing — no matter how small.

END-OF-DAY REFLECTION

What happened today? What did I feel? What do I carry into tomorrow?

ENERGY LEVEL TODAY

☐ 1　☐ 2　☐ 3　☐ 4　☐ 5

Low　　　High

DID I SHOW UP TODAY?

☐ Yes　☐ No — and that's okay.

Tomorrow is a new day.

DAY 69

Date:

of 100

TODAY'S INTENTION

In one sentence — what am I here to do today?

MY 100-MINUTE BLOCK

Block 1	**Block 2**	**Block 3**	**Block 4**
25 min	*25 min*	*25 min*	*25 min*
☐ Complete	☐ Complete	☐ Complete	☐ Complete

TODAY'S WIN

One thing — no matter how small.

END-OF-DAY REFLECTION

What happened today? What did I feel? What do I carry into tomorrow?

ENERGY LEVEL TODAY

☐ 1 ☐ 2 ☐ 3 ☐ 4 ☐ 5

Low   High

DID I SHOW UP TODAY?

☐ Yes   ☐ No — and that's okay.

Tomorrow is a new day.

DAY 70

Date:

of 100

TODAY'S INTENTION

In one sentence — what am I here to do today?

MY 100-MINUTE BLOCK

Block 1	Block 2	Block 3	Block 4
25 min	*25 min*	*25 min*	*25 min*
☐ Complete	☐ Complete	☐ Complete	☐ Complete

TODAY'S WIN

One thing — no matter how small.

END-OF-DAY REFLECTION

What happened today? What did I feel? What do I carry into tomorrow?

ENERGY LEVEL TODAY

☐ 1 ☐ 2 ☐ 3 ☐ 4 ☐ 5

Low   High

DID I SHOW UP TODAY?

☐ Yes   ☐ No — and that's okay.

Tomorrow is a new day.

DAY 71

Date:

of 100

TODAY'S INTENTION

In one sentence — what am I here to do today?

MY 100-MINUTE BLOCK

Block 1 25 min	**Block 2** 25 min	**Block 3** 25 min	**Block 4** 25 min
☐ Complete	☐ Complete	☐ Complete	☐ Complete

TODAY'S WIN

One thing — no matter how small.

END-OF-DAY REFLECTION

What happened today? What did I feel? What do I carry into tomorrow?

ENERGY LEVEL TODAY

☐ 1　☐ 2　☐ 3　☐ 4　☐ 5

Low　　　High

DID I SHOW UP TODAY?

☐ Yes　☐ No — and that's okay.

Tomorrow's a new day.

DAY 72

Date:

of 100

TODAY'S INTENTION

In one sentence — what am I here to do today?

MY 100-MINUTE BLOCK

Block 1	**Block 2**	**Block 3**	**Block 4**
25 min	*25 min*	*25 min*	*25 min*
☐ Complete	☐ Complete	☐ Complete	☐ Complete

TODAY'S WIN

One thing — no matter how small.

END-OF-DAY REFLECTION

What happened today? What did I feel? What do I carry into tomorrow?

ENERGY LEVEL TODAY

☐ 1 ☐ 2 ☐ 3 ☐ 4 ☐ 5

Low   High

DID I SHOW UP TODAY?

☐ Yes   ☐ No — and that's okay.

Tomorrow is a new day.

DAY 73

Date:

of 100

TODAY'S INTENTION

In one sentence — what am I here to do today?

MY 100-MINUTE BLOCK

Block 1	**Block 2**	**Block 3**	**Block 4**
25 min	25 min	25 min	25 min
☐ Complete	☐ Complete	☐ Complete	☐ Complete

TODAY'S WIN

One thing — no matter how small.

END-OF-DAY REFLECTION

What happened today? What did I feel? What do I carry into tomorrow?

ENERGY LEVEL TODAY

☐ 1 ☐ 2 ☐ 3 ☐ 4 ☐ 5

Low   High

DID I SHOW UP TODAY?

☐ Yes   ☐ No — and that's okay.

Tomorrow is a new day.

DAY 74

Date:

of 100

TODAY'S INTENTION

In one sentence — what am I here to do today?

MY 100-MINUTE BLOCK

Block 1	Block 2	Block 3	Block 4
25 min	*25 min*	*25 min*	*25 min*
☐ Complete	☐ Complete	☐ Complete	☐ Complete

TODAY'S WIN

One thing — no matter how small.

END-OF-DAY REFLECTION

What happened today? What did I feel? What do I carry into tomorrow?

ENERGY LEVEL TODAY

☐ 1 ☐ 2 ☐ 3 ☐ 4 ☐ 5

Low   High

DID I SHOW UP TODAY?

☐ Yes   ☐ No — and that's okay.

Tomorrow is a new day.

DAY 75

"*Seventy-five days. Most people never make it here. You are not most people. Twenty-five days stand between you and something you will carry for the rest of your life.*"

THE HOME STRETCH — DO NOT SLOW DOWN NOW

THE 100 METHOD™

DAY 75 OF 100

MILESTONE CHECK-IN

Date:

AM I STILL ALIGNED WITH MY ORIGINAL GOAL? WHAT HAS SHIFTED?

WHAT HAS CHANGED IN ME SO FAR — EVEN IF I CAN'T FULLY SEE IT YET?

WHAT DO I NEED TO RELEASE OR ADJUST GOING FORWARD?

ONE THING I'M PROUD OF THAT I DIDN'T EXPECT:

MY INTENTION FOR THE NEXT 25 DAYS:

"75 days in. Keep going. The best is still ahead."

DAY 76

Date:

of 100

TODAY'S INTENTION

In one sentence — what am I here to do today?

MY 100-MINUTE BLOCK

Block 1	Block 2	Block 3	Block 4
25 min	25 min	25 min	25 min
☐ Complete	☐ Complete	☐ Complete	☐ Complete

TODAY'S WIN

One thing — no matter how small.

END-OF-DAY REFLECTION

What happened today? What did I feel? What do I carry into tomorrow?

ENERGY LEVEL TODAY

☐ 1 ☐ 2 ☐ 3 ☐ 4 ☐ 5

Low   High

DID I SHOW UP TODAY?

☐ Yes   ☐ No — and that's okay.

Tomorrow is a new day.

DAY 77

Date:

of 100

TODAY'S INTENTION

In one sentence — what am I here to do today?

MY 100-MINUTE BLOCK

Block 1	Block 2	Block 3	Block 4
25 min	*25 min*	*25 min*	*25 min*
☐ Complete	☐ Complete	☐ Complete	☐ Complete

TODAY'S WIN

One thing — no matter how small.

END-OF-DAY REFLECTION

What happened today? What did I feel? What do I carry into tomorrow?

ENERGY LEVEL TODAY

☐ 1 ☐ 2 ☐ 3 ☐ 4 ☐ 5

Low　　　　High

DID I SHOW UP TODAY?

☐ Yes　☐ No — and that's okay.

Tomorrow is a new day.

DAY 78

Date:

of 100

TODAY'S INTENTION

In one sentence — what am I here to do today?

MY 100-MINUTE BLOCK

	Block 1	**Block 2**	**Block 3**	**Block 4**
	25 min	25 min	25 min	25 min
	☐ Complete	☐ Complete	☐ Complete	☐ Complete

TODAY'S WIN

One thing — no matter how small.

END-OF-DAY REFLECTION

What happened today? What did I feel? What do I carry into tomorrow?

ENERGY LEVEL TODAY

☐ 1 ☐ 2 ☐ 3 ☐ 4 ☐ 5

Low   High

DID I SHOW UP TODAY?

☐ Yes   ☐ No — and that's okay.

Tomorrow is a new day.

DAY 79

Date:

of 100

TODAY'S INTENTION

In one sentence — what am I here to do today?

MY 100-MINUTE BLOCK

Block 1	Block 2	Block 3	Block 4
25 min	*25 min*	*25 min*	*25 min*
☐ Complete	☐ Complete	☐ Complete	☐ Complete

TODAY'S WIN

One thing — no matter how small.

END-OF-DAY REFLECTION

What happened today? What did I feel? What do I carry into tomorrow?

ENERGY LEVEL TODAY

☐ 1 ☐ 2 ☐ 3 ☐ 4 ☐ 5

Low   High

DID I SHOW UP TODAY?

☐ Yes   ☐ No — and that's okay.

Tomorrow is a new day.

DAY 80

Date:

of 100

TODAY'S INTENTION

In one sentence — what am I here to do today?

MY 100-MINUTE BLOCK

Block 1	Block 2	Block 3	Block 4
25 min	25 min	25 min	25 min
☐ Complete	☐ Complete	☐ Complete	☐ Complete

TODAY'S WIN

One thing — no matter how small.

END-OF-DAY REFLECTION

What happened today? What did I feel? What do I carry into tomorrow?

ENERGY LEVEL TODAY

☐ 1 ☐ 2 ☐ 3 ☐ 4 ☐ 5

Low   High

DID I SHOW UP TODAY?

☐ Yes   ☐ No — and that's okay.

Tomorrow is a new day.

DAY 81

Date:

of 100

TODAY'S INTENTION

In one sentence — what am I here to do today?

MY 100-MINUTE BLOCK

Block 1	Block 2	Block 3	Block 4
25 min	*25 min*	*25 min*	*25 min*
☐ Complete	☐ Complete	☐ Complete	☐ Complete

TODAY'S WIN

One thing — no matter how small.

END-OF-DAY REFLECTION

What happened today? What did I feel? What do I carry into tomorrow?

ENERGY LEVEL TODAY

☐ 1　☐ 2　☐ 3　☐ 4　☐ 5

Low　　　　High

DID I SHOW UP TODAY?

☐ Yes　☐ No — and that's okay.

Tomorrow is a new day.

DAY 82

Date:

of 100

TODAY'S INTENTION

In one sentence — what am I here to do today?

MY 100-MINUTE BLOCK

Block 1	**Block 2**	**Block 3**	**Block 4**
25 min	25 min	25 min	25 min
☐ Complete	☐ Complete	☐ Complete	☐ Complete

TODAY'S WIN

One thing — no matter how small.

END-OF-DAY REFLECTION

What happened today? What did I feel? What do I carry into tomorrow?

ENERGY LEVEL TODAY

☐ 1 ☐ 2 ☐ 3 ☐ 4 ☐ 5

Low   High

DID I SHOW UP TODAY?

☐ Yes   ☐ No — and that's okay.

Tomorrow is a new day.

DAY 83

Date:

of 100

TODAY'S INTENTION

In one sentence — what am I here to do today?

MY 100-MINUTE BLOCK

Block 1	Block 2	Block 3	Block 4
25 min	*25 min*	*25 min*	*25 min*
☐ Complete	☐ Complete	☐ Complete	☐ Complete

TODAY'S WIN

One thing — no matter how small.

END-OF-DAY REFLECTION

What happened today? What did I feel? What do I carry into tomorrow?

ENERGY LEVEL TODAY

☐ 1 ☐ 2 ☐ 3 ☐ 4 ☐ 5

Low   High

DID I SHOW UP TODAY?

☐ Yes   ☐ No — and that's okay.

Tomorrow is a new day.

DAY 84

Date:

of 100

TODAY'S INTENTION

In one sentence — what am I here to do today?

MY 100-MINUTE BLOCK

Block 1 25 min	**Block 2** 25 min	**Block 3** 25 min	**Block 4** 25 min
☐ Complete	☐ Complete	☐ Complete	☐ Complete

TODAY'S WIN

One thing — no matter how small.

END-OF-DAY REFLECTION

What happened today? What did I feel? What do I carry into tomorrow?

ENERGY LEVEL TODAY

☐ 1 ☐ 2 ☐ 3 ☐ 4 ☐ 5

Low   High

DID I SHOW UP TODAY?

☐ Yes   ☐ No — and that's okay.

Tomorrow is a new day.

DAY 85

Date:

of 100

TODAY'S INTENTION

In one sentence — what am I here to do today?

MY 100-MINUTE BLOCK

Block 1	Block 2	Block 3	Block 4
25 min	*25 min*	*25 min*	*25 min*
☐ Complete	☐ Complete	☐ Complete	☐ Complete

TODAY'S WIN

One thing — no matter how small.

END-OF-DAY REFLECTION

What happened today? What did I feel? What do I carry into tomorrow?

ENERGY LEVEL TODAY

☐ 1 ☐ 2 ☐ 3 ☐ 4 ☐ 5

Low　　　　High

DID I SHOW UP TODAY?

☐ Yes　☐ No — and that's okay.

Tomorrow is a new day.

DAY 86

Date:

of 100

TODAY'S INTENTION

In one sentence — what am I here to do today?

MY 100-MINUTE BLOCK

Block 1 25 min	**Block 2** 25 min	**Block 3** 25 min	**Block 4** 25 min
☐ Complete	☐ Complete	☐ Complete	☐ Complete

TODAY'S WIN

One thing — no matter how small.

END-OF-DAY REFLECTION

What happened today? What did I feel? What do I carry into tomorrow?

ENERGY LEVEL TODAY

☐ 1 ☐ 2 ☐ 3 ☐ 4 ☐ 5

Low　　　　　High

DID I SHOW UP TODAY?

☐ Yes　☐ No — and that's okay.

Tomorrow is a new day.

DAY 87

Date:

of 100

TODAY'S INTENTION

In one sentence — what am I here to do today?

MY 100-MINUTE BLOCK

Block 1	Block 2	Block 3	Block 4
25 min	*25 min*	*25 min*	*25 min*
☐ Complete	☐ Complete	☐ Complete	☐ Complete

TODAY'S WIN

One thing -- no matter how small.

END-OF-DAY REFLECTION

What happened today? What did I feel? What do I carry into tomorrow?

ENERGY LEVEL TODAY

☐ 1 ☐ 2 ☐ 3 ☐ 4 ☐ 5

Low   High

DID I SHOW UP TODAY?

☐ Yes ☐ No — and that's okay.

Tomorrow is a new day.

DAY 88

Date:

of 100

TODAY'S INTENTION

In one sentence — what am I here to do today?

MY 100-MINUTE BLOCK

Block 1	**Block 2**	**Block 3**	**Block 4**
25 min	25 min	25 min	25 min
☐ Complete	☐ Complete	☐ Complete	☐ Complete

TODAY'S WIN

One thing — no matter how small.

END-OF-DAY REFLECTION

What happened today? What did I feel? What do I carry into tomorrow?

ENERGY LEVEL TODAY

☐ 1　☐ 2　☐ 3　☐ 4　☐ 5

Low　　　　　　High

DID I SHOW UP TODAY?

☐ Yes　☐ No — and that's okay.

Tomorrow is a new start.

DAY 89

Date:

of 100

TODAY'S INTENTION

In one sentence — what am I here to do today?

MY 100-MINUTE BLOCK

Block 1	Block 2	Block 3	Block 4
25 min	*25 min*	*25 min*	*25 min*
☐ Complete	☐ Complete	☐ Complete	☐ Complete

TODAY'S WIN

One thing — no matter how small.

END-OF-DAY REFLECTION

What happened today? What did I feel? What do I carry into tomorrow?

ENERGY LEVEL TODAY

☐ 1 ☐ 2 ☐ 3 ☐ 4 ☐ 5

Low　　　　High

DID I SHOW UP TODAY?

☐ Yes ☐ No — and that's okay.

Tomorrow is a new day.

DAY 90

Date:

of 100

TODAY'S INTENTION

In one sentence — what am I here to do today?

MY 100-MINUTE BLOCK

Block 1	Block 2	Block 3	Block 4
25 min	25 min	25 min	25 min
☐ Complete	☐ Complete	☐ Complete	☐ Complete

TODAY'S WIN

One thing — no matter how small.

END-OF-DAY REFLECTION

What happened today? What did I feel? What do I carry into tomorrow?

ENERGY LEVEL TODAY

☐ 1 ☐ 2 ☐ 3 ☐ 4 ☐ 5

Low   High

DID I SHOW UP TODAY?

☐ Yes   ☐ No — and that's okay.

That's one more than a day

DAY 91

Date:

of 100

TODAY'S INTENTION

In one sentence — what am I here to do today?

MY 100-MINUTE BLOCK

Block 1	Block 2	Block 3	Block 4
25 min	*25 min*	*25 min*	*25 min*
☐ Complete	☐ Complete	☐ Complete	☐ Complete

TODAY'S WIN

One thing — no matter how small.

END-OF-DAY REFLECTION

What happened today? What did I feel? What do I carry into tomorrow?

ENERGY LEVEL TODAY

☐ 1 ☐ 2 ☐ 3 ☐ 4 ☐ 5

Low   High

DID I SHOW UP TODAY?

☐ Yes   ☐ No — and that's okay.

Tomorrow is a new day.

DAY 92

Date:

of 100

TODAY'S INTENTION

In one sentence — what am I here to do today?

MY 100-MINUTE BLOCK

Block 1	Block 2	Block 3	Block 4
25 min	25 min	25 min	25 min
☐ Complete	☐ Complete	☐ Complete	☐ Complete

TODAY'S WIN

One thing — no matter how small.

END-OF-DAY REFLECTION

What happened today? What did I feel? What do I carry into tomorrow?

ENERGY LEVEL TODAY

☐ 1 ☐ 2 ☐ 3 ☐ 4 ☐ 5

Low   High

DID I SHOW UP TODAY?

☐ Yes   ☐ No — and that's okay.

Tomorrow is a new day.

DAY 93

Date:

of 100

TODAY'S INTENTION

In one sentence — what am I here to do today?

MY 100-MINUTE BLOCK

Block 1 25 min	Block 2 25 min	Block 3 25 min	Block 4 25 min
☐ Complete	☐ Complete	☐ Complete	☐ Complete

TODAY'S WIN

One thing — no matter how small.

END-OF-DAY REFLECTION

What happened today? What did I feel? What do I carry into tomorrow?

ENERGY LEVEL TODAY

☐ 1 ☐ 2 ☐ 3 ☐ 4 ☐ 5

Low   High

DID I SHOW UP TODAY?

☐ Yes   ☐ No — and that's okay.

Tomorrow is a new day.

DAY 94

Date:

of 100

TODAY'S INTENTION

In one sentence — what am I here to do today?

MY 100-MINUTE BLOCK

Block 1	Block 2	Block 3	Block 4
25 min	25 min	25 min	25 min
☐ Complete	☐ Complete	☐ Complete	☐ Complete

TODAY'S WIN

One thing — no matter how small.

END-OF-DAY REFLECTION

What happened today? What did I feel? What do I carry into tomorrow?

ENERGY LEVEL TODAY

☐ 1 ☐ 2 ☐ 3 ☐ 4 ☐ 5

Low   High

DID I SHOW UP TODAY?

☐ Yes ☐ No — and that's okay.

Tomorrow's a new day.

DAY 95

Date:

of 100

TODAY'S INTENTION

In one sentence — what am I here to do today?

MY 100-MINUTE BLOCK

Block 1	**Block 2**	**Block 3**	**Block 4**
25 min	*25 min*	*25 min*	*25 min*
☐ Complete	☐ Complete	☐ Complete	☐ Complete

TODAY'S WIN

One thing -- no matter how small.

END-OF-DAY REFLECTION

What happened today? What did I feel? What do I carry into tomorrow?

ENERGY LEVEL TODAY

☐ 1　☐ 2　☐ 3　☐ 4　☐ 5

Low　　　　　High

DID I SHOW UP TODAY?

☐ Yes　☐ No — and that's okay.

Tomorrow is a new day.

DAY 96

Date:

of 100

TODAY'S INTENTION

In one sentence — what am I here to do today?

MY 100-MINUTE BLOCK

Block 1	**Block 2**	**Block 3**	**Block 4**
25 min	25 min	25 min	25 min
☐ Complete	☐ Complete	☐ Complete	☐ Complete

TODAY'S WIN

One thing — no matter how small.

END-OF-DAY REFLECTION

What happened today? What did I feel? What do I carry into tomorrow?

ENERGY LEVEL TODAY

☐ 1 ☐ 2 ☐ 3 ☐ 4 ☐ 5

Low   High

DID I SHOW UP TODAY?

☐ Yes   ☐ No — and that's okay.

Tomorrow is a new day.

DAY 97

Date:

of 100

TODAY'S INTENTION

In one sentence — what am I here to do today?

MY 100-MINUTE BLOCK

Block 1 *25 min*	**Block 2** *25 min*	**Block 3** *25 min*	**Block 4** *25 min*
☐ Complete	☐ Complete	☐ Complete	☐ Complete

TODAY'S WIN

One thing — no matter how small.

END-OF-DAY REFLECTION

What happened today? What did I feel? What do I carry into tomorrow?

ENERGY LEVEL TODAY

☐ 1 ☐ 2 ☐ 3 ☐ 4 ☐ 5

Low　　　　　High

DID I SHOW UP TODAY?

☐ Yes   ☐ No — and that's okay.

Tomorrow is a new day.

DAY 98

Date:

of 100

TODAY'S INTENTION

In one sentence — what am I here to do today?

MY 100-MINUTE BLOCK

Block 1	Block 2	Block 3	Block 4
25 min	25 min	25 min	25 min
☐ Complete	☐ Complete	☐ Complete	☐ Complete

TODAY'S WIN

One thing — no matter how small.

END-OF-DAY REFLECTION

What happened today? What did I feel? What do I carry into tomorrow?

ENERGY LEVEL TODAY

☐ 1 ☐ 2 ☐ 3 ☐ 4 ☐ 5

Low   High

DID I SHOW UP TODAY?

☐ Yes   ☐ No — and that's okay.

Tomorrow is a new day.

DAY 99

Date:

of 100

TODAY'S INTENTION

In one sentence — what am I here to do today?

MY 100-MINUTE BLOCK

Block 1	Block 2	Block 3	Block 4
25 min	*25 min*	*25 min*	*25 min*
☐ Complete	☐ Complete	☐ Complete	☐ Complete

TODAY'S WIN

One thing — no matter how small.

END-OF-DAY REFLECTION

What happened today? What did I feel? What do I carry into tomorrow?

ENERGY LEVEL TODAY

☐ 1 ☐ 2 ☐ 3 ☐ 4 ☐ 5

Low   High

DID I SHOW UP TODAY?

☐ Yes ☐ No — and that's okay.

Tomorrow is a new day.

DAY 100

"One hundred days. One hundred minutes. One goal. You kept your word to the most important person in your life — yourself. This is what becoming looks like."

DAY 100.

YOU SHOWED UP. YOU FINISHED.

100 Minutes. 100 Days. 1 Goal. Complete.

WHAT DID I ACCOMPLISH OVER THESE 100 DAYS?

WHAT DID I LEARN ABOUT MYSELF IN THIS PROCESS?

WHAT ARE MY NEXT STEPS FROM HERE?

WHAT CHANGES, IF ANY, WILL I MAKE TO MY ROUTINE GOING FORWARD?

WHO DO I WANT TO THANK OR ACKNOWLEDGE?

"You did not just complete a goal. You became someone who finishes what they start."

Who I Was vs. Who I Am

Go back to your Starting Point page. Read what you wrote. Now answer the same questions — honestly. The distance between those two answers is your transformation.

DAY 1 — WHO I WAS	DAY 100 — WHO I AM
Physically:	Physically:
Mentally & Emotionally:	Mentally & Emotionally:
Daily Routine:	Daily Routine:
My Belief in Myself:	My Belief in Myself:

My Next 100

You know how this works now. You know what 100 minutes a day can do. The only question is — what's next?

MY NEXT GOAL:

WHY THIS GOAL, WHY NOW?

WHAT I WILL DO DIFFERENTLY THIS TIME BASED ON WHAT I LEARNED:

MY START DATE FOR THE NEXT 100:

"Growth doesn't stop at 100. It's just getting started."

A Letter to You

When you first opened this planner, you made a decision. Maybe it felt small in the moment — just picking something up, just filling out a name on a page. But that decision was the beginning of everything that followed.

You showed up on the days when you were motivated. You showed up on the days when you weren't. You showed up when life got in the way, when doubt crept in, when the goal felt far away. And that — more than the result — is the real achievement.

The world is full of people who start things. What you have just proven is that you are someone who finishes. That is rare. That matters. That changes the story you tell about yourself.

The 100 Method was never just about 100 minutes a day. It was about proving to yourself — one day at a time — that you are worth showing up for. That your goals are worth fighting for. That the person you are becoming is worth the effort.

You did the work.

You kept your word.

You became someone new.

Now go build your next 100.

— The 100 Method

YOUR SPACE

NOTES

NOTES

NOTES

YOUR SPACE

NOTES

YOUR SPACE

NOTES

YOUR SPACE

NOTES

www.ingramcontent.com/pod-product-compliance
Lightning Source LLC
Chambersburg PA
CBHW081956260726
48659CB00009BA/2865